# Contents

The *All-Star Math* series of books offers parents and educators a unique approach to teaching foundational math concepts to children in a way they will truly enjoy. *All-Star Math* presents children with high-interest problems that they will want to learn to solve.

The lessons seamlessly integrate the national standards and skills required for children to develop math proficiency on many levels. Correlations of the lessons to the National Council for the Teaching of Mathematics (NCTM) standards are on pages 4–5. Standards include:

- Number Computation
- Geometry and Spatial Sense
- Algebra
- Measurement
- Patterns and Relationships
- Fractions and Decimals

All-Star Math, *Grades 1–2*, contains 9 units and 44 lessons.

- Unit 1, Number Sense, introduces children to basic number concepts.
- Unit 2, Addition, teaches basic ways to add numbers.
- Unit 3, Subtraction, shows children subtraction and how to use fact families.
- Unit 4, Place Value, explains to children the importance of what a numeral means in a number and in comparison to other numbers.
- Unit 5, Geometry and Patterns, teaches children the names and characteristics of basic shapes and patterns.
- Unit 6, Measurement and Fractions, involves children in measuring length, weight, volume, and temperature and helps children identify fractions that are part of a whole and part of a group.
- Unit 7, Time and Money, uses clocks, calendars, and money to teach basic time measurement and money values.
- Unit 8, Multiplication and Division, introduces multiplication for combining groups and division for separating groups.
- Unit 9, Data and Analysis, shows children how to use tables and graphs and how to determine probability.

The components of each *All-Star Math* two-page lesson are:

The **problem** presents a sports math problem that needs a solution.

Think About It guides children through a five-step process to think about how to solve the problem.

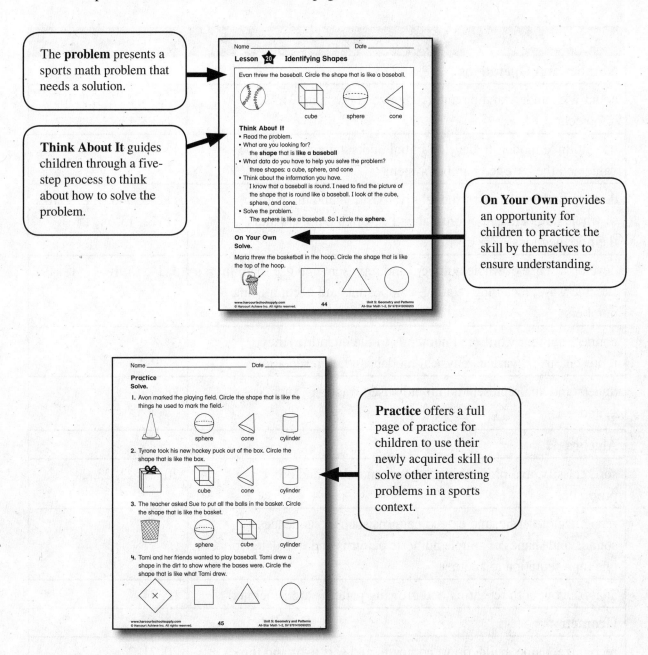

On Your Own provides an opportunity for children to practice the skill by themselves to ensure understanding.

Practice offers a full page of practice for children to use their newly acquired skill to solve other interesting problems in a sports context.

An **Answer Key** on pages 94–96 is included to make sure the answers to all the **On Your Own** and **Practice** problems are correct.

All-Star Math 1–2, SV 9781419099205

Standards/Correlations

Correlation to NCTM Standards

Content Strand	Lesson
Number and Operations	
count with understanding and recognize "how many" in sets of objects	1, 2, 3, 4, 7, 8, 9, 10, 11, 12, 13
use multiple models to develop initial understandings of place value and the base-ten number system	16, 17
develop understanding of the relative position and magnitude of whole numbers and of ordinal and cardinal numbers and their connections	1, 2, 3, 5, 6, 7, 8, 9, 10, 11, 12, 13, 14, 15
develop a sense of whole numbers and represent and use them in flexible ways, including relating, composing, and decomposing numbers	3, 14, 15, 16, 17, 18, 19
connect number words and numerals to the quantities they represent, using various physical models and representations	3
understand and represent commonly used fractions, such as $\frac{1}{4}$, $\frac{1}{3}$, and $\frac{1}{2}$	28, 29
Algebra	
sort, classify, and order objects by size, number, and other properties	20, 21, 22, 23, 24
recognize, describe, and extend patterns such as sequences of sounds and shapes or simple numeric patterns and translate from one representation to another	18, 24
analyze how both repeating and growing patterns are generated	18, 24
Geometry	
recognize, name, build, draw, compare, and sort two- and three-dimensional shapes	20, 21, 22, 23, 24
describe attributes and parts of two- and three-dimensional shapes	20, 21, 22, 23, 24
investigate and predict the results of putting together and taking apart two- and three-dimensional shapes	20, 21, 22, 23, 24

Content Strand	Lesson
Measurement	
recognize the attributes of length, volume, weight, area, and time	25, 26, 27, 30, 31
compare and order objects according to these attributes	25, 26, 27, 30, 31
understand how to measure using nonstandard and standard units	25, 26
select an appropriate unit and tool for the attribute being measured	25, 26, 27, 30, 31
Data Analysis and Probability	
pose questions and gather data about themselves and their surroundings	40, 41, 42, 43, 44
sort and classify objects according to their attributes and organize data about the objects	40, 41, 42, 43, 44
represent data using concrete objects, pictures, and graphs	40, 41, 42

Name _____   Date _____

Lesson Numbers Through 10

Jim's baseball team needs 9 players. Color 9 of the players.

Think About It

• Read the problem.
• What are you looking for?

   9 players

• What data do you have to help you solve the problem?

   10 players

• Think about the information you have.

   I know that Jim's baseball team needs 9 players. I need to count the number of players in the picture.

• Solve the problem.

   So I count and color **9 baseball players**.

On Your Own
Solve.

Pam's basketball team has 5 players. Color 5 of the players.

All-Star Math 1–2, SV 9781419099205

Name _____   Date _____

Practice
Solve.

1. Jill has 6 players on her soccer team. Color 6 of the players.

2. Jamal shot 3 arrows into the target. Color 3 arrows.

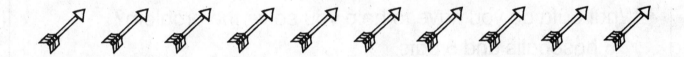

3. Lee needed 4 paddles to play table tennis with his friends. Color 4 paddles.

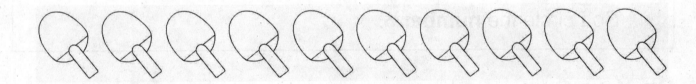

4. In bowling, there are 10 pins in the lane. Color 10 pins.

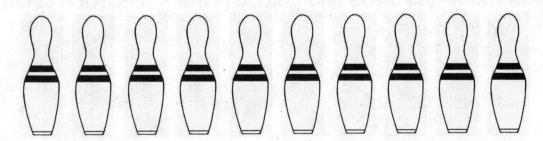

All-Star Math 1–2, SV 9781419099205

Name _____ Date _____

Lesson **2**   Comparing Numbers

Write how many baseballs and bats there are. Then circle the number that is greater.

_____

Think About It

- Read the problem.
- What are you looking for?

    the number of **baseballs and bats** and the **greater** number
- What data do you have to help you solve the problem?

    6 baseballs and 5 bats
- Think about the information you have.

    I count 6 baseballs and 5 bats. I write the numbers 6 and 5.

    I know that 6 comes after 5. So 6 is greater than 5.
- Solve the problem.

    So I circle the **number 6**.

On Your Own
Solve.

Write how many golf clubs and golf balls there are. Then circle the number that is greater.

_____

All-Star Math 1–2, SV 9781419099205

Name _____   Date _____

Practice
Solve.

1. Write how many speedboats and race cars there are. Then circle the number that is less.

_____   _____

2. Write how many sleds and bowling balls there are. Then circle the number that is greater.

_____   _____

3. Write how many tennis shoes and footballs there are. Then circle the number that is less.

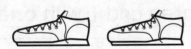   

_____   _____

4. Write how many boxing gloves and tennis rackets there are. Then circle the number that is greater.

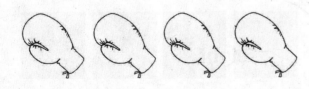

_____   _____

All-Star Math 1–2, SV 9781419099205

Name _____   Date _____

Lesson Matching Numbers and Words

Draw lines to connect the numbers to the correct number words.

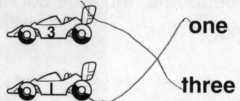

Think About It

- Read the problem.
- What are you looking for?

  the **numbers on the cars** and their correct **number words**

- What data do you have to help you solve the problem?

  3 race cars with numbers and 3 number words

- Think about the information you have.

  I know the numbers on the cars are 3 and 1. I know the
  number words are one and three. I need to draw lines to
  connect the numbers with the correct number words.

- Solve the problem.

  So I draw lines to connect <u>3</u> with **three** and <u>1</u> with **one**.

On Your Own
Solve.

Draw lines to connect the numbers to the correct number words.

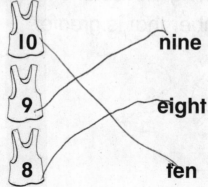

All-Star Math 1–2, SV 9781419099205

Practice
Solve.

Draw lines to connect the numbers to the correct number words.

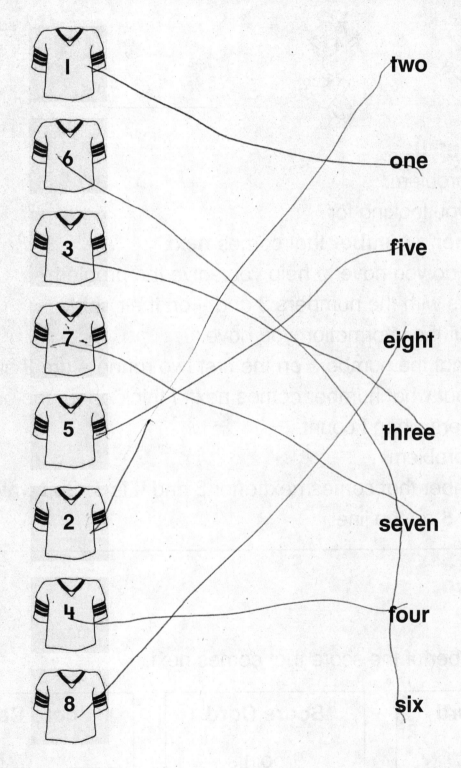

1	two
6	one
3	five
7	eight
5	three
2	seven
4	four
8	six

Unit 1: Number Sense
All-Star Math 1–2, SV 9781419099205

Name _____ Date _____

Lesson ⭐4 Ordering Numbers

Write the runner's number that comes next.

_____

Think About It

- Read the problem.
- What are you looking for?

  the **runner's number** that comes **next**
- What data do you have to help you solve the problem?

  2 runners with the numbers 3 and 4 on their shirts
- Think about the information you have.

  I know that the numbers on the first two runners are 3 and 4.

  To find out what number comes next, I think about the order

  of numbers when I count.
- Solve the problem.

  The number that comes next after 3 and 4 is 5. So I write the

  number 5 on the line.

On Your Own
Solve.

Write the number of the score that comes next.

Score Card	Score Card	Score Card
8 points	9 points	_____ points

Name _____   Date _____

Practice
Solve.

Write the missing numbers on the flags in the correct order.

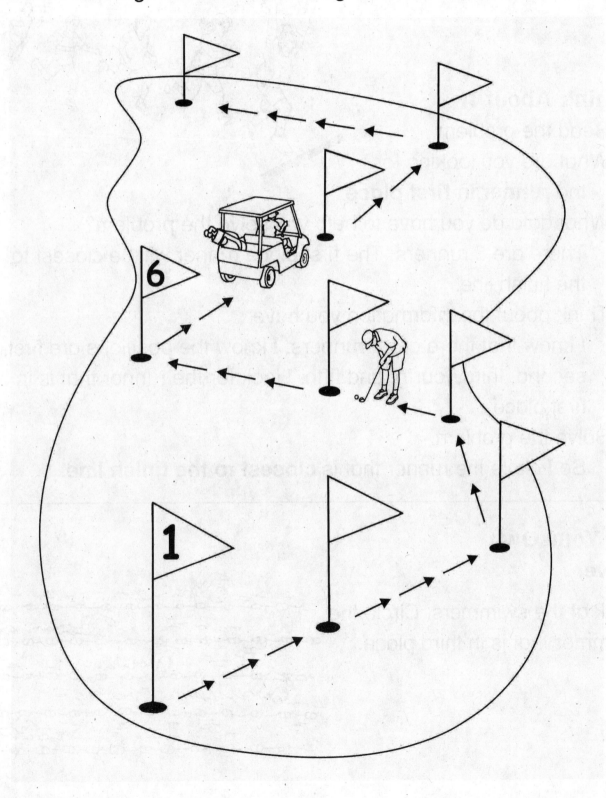

Name _____ Date _____

Lesson Ordinal Numbers

Look at the runners. Circle the runner that is in first place.

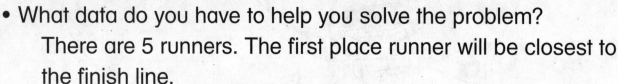

Think About It
- Read the problem.
- What are you looking for?
  the **runner in first place**
- What data do you have to help you solve the problem?
  There are 5 runners. The first place runner will be closest to the finish line.
- Think about the information you have.
  I know that there are 5 runners. I know the positions are first, second, third, fourth, and fifth. I look for the runner that is in first place.
- Solve the problem.
  So I circle the runner that is **closest to the finish line**.

On Your Own
Solve.

Look at the swimmers. Circle the swimmer that is in third place.

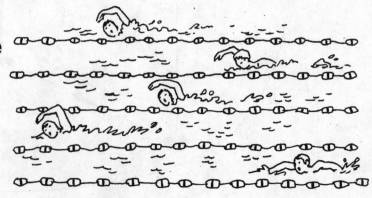

All-Star Math 1–2, SV 9781419099205

Name _____ Date _____

Practice
Solve.

1. Look at the race cars. Circle the race car that is in second place.

2. Look at the batters waiting in line for their turn to bat. Circle the batter that is fifth in line.

3. Look at the jumpers waiting in line. Circle the jumper that is fourth in line.

4. Look at the children in line to buy tickets to a football game. Circle the child that is first in line.

Name _____ Date _____

Lesson 6   Adding 0, 1, and 2

Ken hit 2 home runs in the first softball game. Then he hit
0 home runs in the second game. How many home runs did
he hit in all?

Think About It

- Read the problem.
- What are you looking for?

    how many **home runs** Ken **hit in all**

- What data do you have to help you solve the problem?

    2 home runs hit in the first game

    0 home runs hit in the second game

- Think about the information you have.

    I know that Ken hit 2 home runs in the first game and 0 home

    runs in the second game. I need to find how many home

    runs he hit in both games. I add to solve the problem.

- Solve the problem.

    2 home runs + 0 home runs = 2 home runs

    So Ken **hit 2 home runs in all**.

On Your Own
Solve.

Kellie played football with some friends. She scored a touchdown
and got 6 points. Then she kicked the extra point for 1 point. How
many points did Kellie get?

All-Star Math 1–2, SV 9781419099205

Name _____ Date _____

Practice
Solve.

1. Zane and his dad went fishing. Zane caught 3 fish in the morning and 0 fish in the afternoon. How many fish did Zane catch in all?

2. Betty skated 3 times around the rink. Then she skated 2 more times around the rink. How many times did Betty skate around the rink in all?

3. Last month Julie won 5 ribbons at a horse show. This month she won 2 ribbons. How many ribbons did Julie win in both months?

4. Lee dived into the pool 4 times yesterday and 1 time today. How many times did Lee dive into the pool both days?

Name _____ Date _____

Lesson 7 Joining Groups

Write the addition sentence.

_____3_____   +   _____6_____   =   _____9_____

Think About It

• Read the problem.
• What are you looking for?
  numbers to write an **addition sentence**
• What data do you have to help you solve the problem?
  3 baseball players
  6 baseball players
• Think about the information you have.
  I know I need to join 2 groups of baseball players. There are
  3 baseball players in the first group. There are 6 baseball
  players in the second group. I add to solve the problem.
• Solve the problem.
  $3 + 6 = 9$
  So the addition sentence is **3 + 6 = 9**.

On Your Own
Solve.

Write the addition sentence.

_____5_____   +   _____7_____   =   _____12_____

www.harcourtschoolsupply.com
© Harcourt Achieve Inc. All rights reserved.   **18**   Unit 2: Addition
All-Star Math 1–2, SV 9781419099205

Name _____   Date _____

Practice
Solve.

1. Write the addition sentence.

___2___ + ___4___ = ___6___

2. Write the addition sentence.

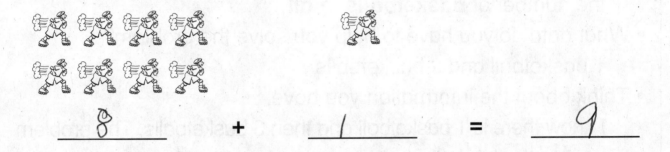

___8___ + ___1___ = ___9___

3. Write the addition sentence.

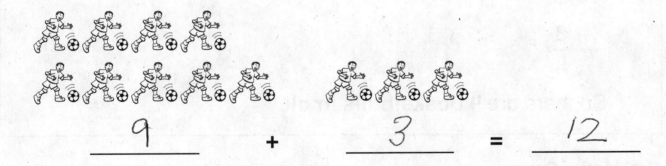

___9___ + ___3___ = ___12___

4. Write the addition sentence.

___4___ + ___4___ = ___8___

Unit 2: Addition
All-Star Math 1–2, SV 9781419099205

Name _____ Date _____

Lesson Vertical Addition

How many basketballs are there in all?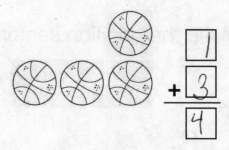

Think About It

- Read the problem.
- What are you looking for?

  the number of **basketballs in all**

- What data do you have to help you solve the problem?

  1 basketball and 3 basketballs

- Think about the information you have.

  I know there is 1 basketball and then 3 basketballs. The problem next to the basketballs shows that I add the two numbers.

- Solve the problem.

$$
\begin{array}{r}
1 \\
+\ 3 \\
\hline
4
\end{array}
$$

  So there are **4 basketballs in all**.

On Your Own
Solve.

How many ice skates are there altogether?

All-Star Math 1–2, SV 9781419099205

Name _____ Date _____

Practice
Solve.

1. How many oars are there altogether?

$$\begin{array}{r} 3 \\ +\ 2 \\ \hline 5 \end{array}$$

2. How many mitts are there in all?

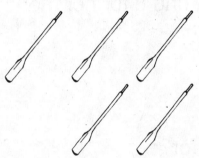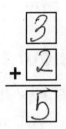

$$\begin{array}{r} 6 \\ +\ 3 \\ \hline 9 \end{array}$$

3. How many targets are there in all?

$$\begin{array}{r} 5 \\ +\ 5 \\ \hline 6 \end{array}$$

4. How many runners are there altogether?

$$\begin{array}{r} 5 \\ +\ 3 \\ \hline 8 \end{array}$$

Lesson Adding 3 Addends

Ginny bought tickets to the tennis match. She bought 1 ticket for her mom, 1 for her dad, and 8 for her friends. How many tickets did Ginny buy in all?

Think About It

ADMIT **1** ONE

• Read the problem.

• What are you looking for?

   the number of **tickets** Ginny **bought in all**

• What data do you have to help you solve the problem?

   1 ticket for mom, 1 ticket for dad, 8 tickets for friends

• Think about the information you have.

   I know that Ginny bought 1 ticket for her mom, 1 ticket for her dad, and 8 tickets for her friends. I need to find how many she bought in all. I add to solve the problem.

• Solve the problem.

$$
\begin{array}{r}
1 \text{ ticket} \\
1 \text{ ticket} \\
+ \ 8 \text{ tickets} \\
\hline
10 \text{ tickets}
\end{array}
$$

So Ginny **bought 10 tickets in all**.

On Your Own
Solve.

Ron's soccer team scored 4 points in the first game, 2 points in the second game, and 2 points in the third game. How many points did Ron's team score in the 3 games?

Name _____ Date _____

Practice
Solve.

1. On Monday, Dave swam 3 laps. On Tuesday, he swam 4 laps. On Wednesday, he swam 3 laps. How many laps did Dave swim over the 3 days?

2. LaToya ran the track at school. She ran 2 laps, 3 laps, and then 3 more laps. How many laps did LaToya run in all?

3. Tran sold tickets to a soccer game. He sold 6 tickets the first week, 4 tickets the second week, and 0 tickets the third week. How many tickets did Tran sell altogether?

4. Dena practiced her jumping for track-and-field day. She jumped 2 feet, 2 feet, and 3 feet. How many feet did Dena jump in all?

All-Star Math 1–2, SV 9781419099205

Name _____ Date _____

Lesson Addition with Regrouping

The Wolves scored 42 points in their first football game. They scored 28 points in their second game. How many points did they score in both games?

Think About It

• Read the problem.
• What are you looking for?
  the number of **points** the Wolves **scored in both games**
• What data do you have to help you solve the problem?
  42 points scored in first game
  28 points scored in second game
• Think about the information you have.
  I know that the Wolves scored 42 points in the first game and 28 points in the second game. I need to find how many points they scored in both games. I add to solve the problem.
• Solve the problem.

$$\begin{array}{r} 42 \text{ points} \\ + \ 28 \text{ points} \\ \hline 70 \text{ points} \end{array}$$

So the Wolves **scored 70 points in both games**.

On Your Own
Solve. Use another sheet of paper.

Doug was getting ready to run in a big race. He ran 15 laps around his yard on Monday. He ran 19 laps on Tuesday. How many laps did he run altogether?

Name _____ Date _____

Practice
Solve.

1. During a game, Celia ran 14 yards with the football. Then she ran another 8 yards. How many yards did Celia run in all?

2. Brian has 23 baseball cards. He bought 9 more. How many baseball cards does Brian have altogether?

3. Tyrone played 18 holes of golf on Friday. On Saturday, he played 9 holes of golf. How many holes of golf did Tyrone play altogether?

4. There are 67 runners behind the starting line. Another 25 runners join them behind the starting line. How many runners are behind the starting line in all?

Name _____   Date _____

Lesson Taking Away

How many baseball players are left? _____

Think About It
- Read the problem.
- What are you looking for?
  the number of **baseball players left**
- What data do you have to help you solve the problem?
  3 baseball players
  1 baseball player leaves
- Think about the information you have.
  I know that there were 3 baseball players. The <u>X</u> on one
  player means that one player has left. I subtract to solve
  the problem.
- Solve the problem.
  3 baseball players − 1 baseball player = 2 baseball players
  So there are **2 baseball players left**.

On Your Own
Solve.

How many skiers are left? _____

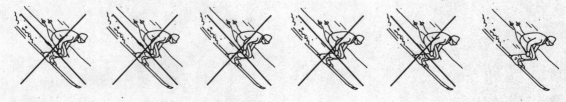

Name _____ Date _____

Practice
Solve.

1. How many bikes are left? _____

2. How many horseback riders are left? _____

3. How many karate students are left? _____

4. How many trophies are left? _____

All-Star Math 1–2, SV 9781419099205

Name _____ Date _____

Lesson 12 Counting Back

Bruce sells baseball caps to make money for his team. He has 5 caps and sells 2. How many caps does Bruce have left? Use the number line. Count back to subtract.

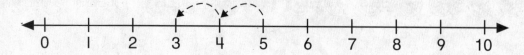

Think About It
- Read the problem.
- What are you looking for?
  the number of **caps** that Bruce has **left**
- What data do you have to help you solve the problem?
  5 caps and 2 caps
- Think about the information you have.
  I know that Bruce has 5 caps to sell. He sells 2 caps. I need to find out how many caps Bruce has left. I subtract to solve the problem. I count back 2 places on the number line.
- Solve the problem.
  5 caps − 2 caps = 3 caps
  So Bruce has **3 caps left**.

On Your Own
Solve.

Mr. Sánchez has 8 horses in his stable. Students are riding 4 of the horses. How many horses are still in the stable? Use the number line. Count back to subtract.

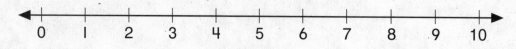

All-Star Math 1–2, SV 9781419099205

Name _____ Date _____

Practice
Solve.

1. Natalie was learning how to play golf. She hit 10 golf balls with her golf club. She lost 2 of the balls. How many golf balls does she have left? Use the number line. Count back to subtract.

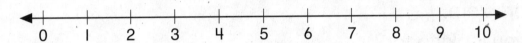

2. There were 7 friends sitting together at a field hockey game. At halftime, 3 of the friends had to leave. The rest of the friends stayed until the end of the game. How many of the friends saw the end of the game? Use the number line. Count back to subtract.

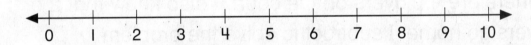

3. Carl tossed 7 horseshoes at a stake. He saw that 2 of the horseshoes he tossed missed the stake. How many horseshoes went around the stake? Use the number line. Count back to subtract.

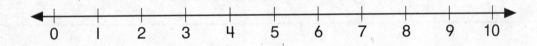

4. There were 9 football players sitting on the bench. Then 2 players left the bench to go on the field. How many players were still on the bench? Use the number line. Count back to subtract.

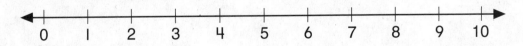

Name _____   Date _____

Lesson Vertical Subtraction

There are 4 tennis players on the court. Then 2 players go home. How many players are left on the court?

Think About It
- Read the problem.
- What are you looking for?

  the number of **tennis players** that are **left** on the court
- What data do you have to help you solve the problem?

  4 players on the court

  2 players go home
- Think about the information you have.

  I know there are 4 players on the court. I also know that 2 of the players go home. I subtract to solve the problem.
- Solve the problem.

  $$\begin{array}{r} 4 \text{ players} \\ -\ 2 \text{ players} \\ \hline 2 \text{ players} \end{array}$$

  So there are **2 tennis players left** on the court.

On Your Own
Solve.

A race had 10 runners. Only 8 of the runners finished the race. How many runners did **NOT** finish the race?

All-Star Math 1–2, SV 9781419099205

Name _____ Date _____

Practice
Solve.

1. Coach Hanson had 15 students sign up to be on his baseball team. There were 6 players that did not make the team. How many players made the team?

2. Brenda rolled the bowling ball at the 10 bowling pins. She knocked down 7 pins. How may pins were left standing?

3. Peggy bought 9 new tennis balls. She gave 3 balls away to her best friend. How many new tennis balls does Peggy have now?

4. Miguel's soccer team had 21 players. The team lost 5 players. How many players were left?

Lesson 14   Fact Families

Add or subtract. Circle the number sentence that does **NOT** belong.

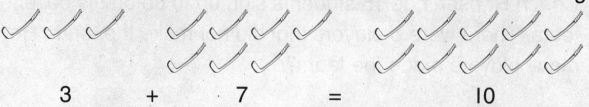

$$3 \quad + \quad 7 \quad = \quad 10$$

7 + 3 = _____   6 + 3 = _____   10 – 7 = _____   10 – 3 = _____

Think About It

- Read the problem.
- What are you looking for?
  the **number sentence** that does **NOT** belong
- What data do you have to help you solve the problem?
  groups of 3, 7, and 10 hockey sticks
- Think about the information you have.
  I know that I should use the numbers 3, 7, and 10. I should
  solve to find the one that does not belong.
- Solve the problems.
  7 + 3 = 10   6 + 3 = 9   10 – 7 = 3   10 – 3 = 7
  So I circle **6 + 3 = 9** because it does **NOT** belong.

On Your Own
Solve.

Add or subtract. Circle the number sentence that does **NOT** belong.

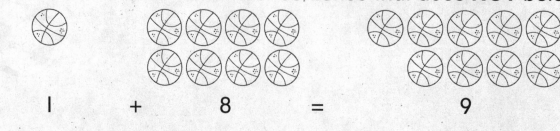

$$1 \quad + \quad 8 \quad = \quad 9$$

8 + 1 = _____   9 – 8 = _____   8 – 1 = _____   9 – 1 = _____

Practice
Solve.

1. Add or subtract. Circle the number sentence that does **NOT** belong.

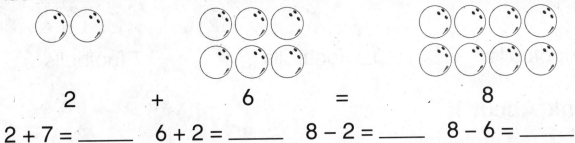

2   +   6   =   8

$2 + 7 =$ _____ $6 + 2 =$ _____ $8 - 2 =$ _____ $8 - 6 =$ _____

2. Add or subtract. Circle the number sentence that does **NOT** belong.

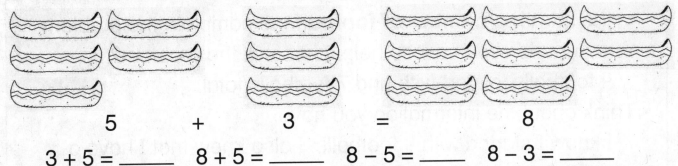

5   +   3   =   8

$3 + 5 =$ _____ $8 + 5 =$ _____ $8 - 5 =$ _____ $8 - 3 =$ _____

3. Add or subtract. Circle the number sentence that does **NOT** belong.

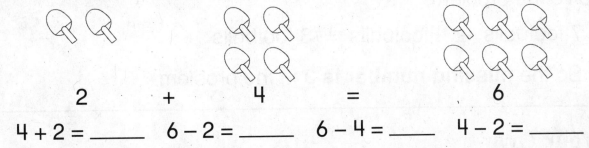

2   +   4   =   6

$4 + 2 =$ _____ $6 - 2 =$ _____ $6 - 4 =$ _____ $4 - 2 =$ _____

4. Add or subtract. Circle the number sentence that does **NOT** belong.

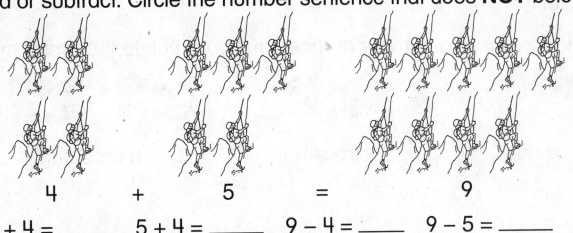

4   +   5   =   9

$9 + 4 =$ _____ $5 + 4 =$ _____ $9 - 4 =$ _____ $9 - 5 =$ _____

All-Star Math 1–2, SV 9781419099205

Name _____   Date _____

Lesson 15   Missing Addends

Fill in the missing number of footballs to complete the problem.

4 footballs   +   __3__ footballs   =   7 footballs

Think About It

- Read the problem.
- What are you looking for?

  the **missing number of footballs** to complete the problem
- What data do you have to help you solve the problem?

  4 footballs to start with and 7 footballs total
- Think about the information you have.

  I know I started with 4 footballs. I also know that I have a total of 7 footballs. I subtract to solve the problem.
- Solve the problem.

  7 footballs − 4 footballs = 3 footballs

  So the **missing number is 3** in the problem.

On Your Own
Solve.

Fill in the missing number of race cars to complete the problem.

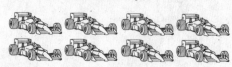

2 race cars   +   __6__ race cars   =   8 race cars

All-Star Math 1–2, SV 9781419099205

Name _____ Date _____

Practice
Solve.

1. Fill in the missing number of bikes to complete the problem.

  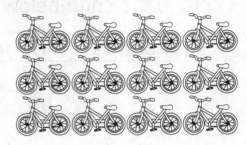

9 bikes   +   __3__ bikes   =   12 bikes

2. Fill in the missing number of horseshoes to complete the problem.

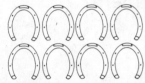 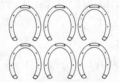 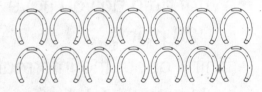

__8__ horseshoes + 6 horseshoes   =   14 horseshoes

3. Fill in the missing number of baseball mitts to complete the problem.

 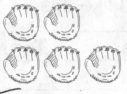 

6 baseball mitts + __5__ baseball mitts   =   11 baseball mitts

4. Fill in the missing number of golf clubs to complete the problem.

  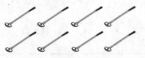

__5__ golf clubs   +   8 golf clubs   =   13 golf clubs

Lesson Ones, Tens, Hundreds, and Thousands

Julien scored 128 points in bowling. Put the numbers of Julien's score in the chart below to show their place value.

Thousands	Hundreds	Tens	Ones

Think About It

- Read the problem.
- What are you looking for?
  the **place value** of Julien's score
- What data do you have to help you solve the problem?
  128 points
- Think about the information you have.
  I know that Julien scored 128 points. I find the place value for each number in 128.
- Solve the problem.
  Julien scored 128 points, which is 1 hundred, 2 tens, and 8 ones. So I fill out the chart like this.

Thousands	Hundreds	Tens	Ones
	1	2	8

On Your Own
Solve.

Dena threw the basketball into the hoop 209 times. Put the numbers of Dena's throws in the chart below to show their place value.

Thousands	Hundreds	Tens	Ones

Practice
Solve.

1. There were 3,204 fans at the football game. Write the number of fans to show their place value.

Thousands	Hundreds	Tens	Ones

2. The number on Donny's race car is 1,826. Place Donny's race car number in the chart to show its place value.

Thousands	Hundreds	Tens	Ones

3. Alton School needed new footballs, basketballs, and soccer balls. To help pay for the new balls, students made $540 selling cupcakes. Put the amount of money the students made in the chart to show its place value.

Thousands	Hundreds	Tens	Ones

4. Frank lifted weights. Yesterday he lifted 68 pounds. Put the number Frank lifted into the chart to show its place value.

Thousands	Hundreds	Tens	Ones

Name _____ Date _____

Lesson After, Before, Between

Look at the football players. Circle the number that comes after 23.

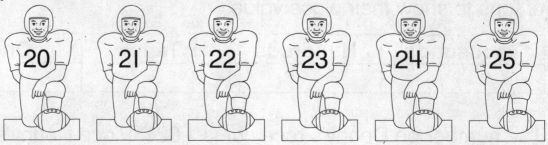

Think About It

• Read the problem.

• What are you looking for?

  the **number** that comes **after 23**

• What data do you have to help you solve the problem?

  the numbers are 20, 21, 22, 23, 24, and 25

• Think about the information you have.

  I know the numbers are in order: 20, 21, 22, 23, 24, and 25.

  I look for the number that comes next after 23.

• Solve the problem.

  The number that comes after 23 is 24. So I circle the

  number 24.

On Your Own
Solve.

Look at the sailboats. Circle the number that comes before 46.

Name _____ Date _____

Practice
Solve.

1. Look at the golf course flags. Circle the number that comes between 9 and 11.

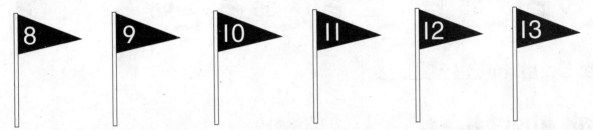

2. Look at the runners in the race. Circle the number that comes between 25 and 27.

3. Look at the horses. Circle the number that comes before 12.

4. Look at the baseball caps. Circle the number that comes after 91.

Name _____ Date _____

Lesson Number Patterns

Look at the pattern. Write the missing numbers. Write a rule.

20   25   ___   35   40   ___

Rule: Count by _____

Think About It

• Read the problem.

• What are you looking for?

  the **missing numbers** and the **rule for the pattern**

• What data do you have to help you solve the problem?

  20, 25, missing number, 35, 40, missing number

• Think about the information you have.

  I know that I would count by 5 to go from 20 to 25 and from 35 to 40. I count by 5s to find the missing numbers.

• Solve the problem.

  I count 20, 25, 30, 35, 40, and 45. So I know the **missing numbers are 30 and 45**. The rule is **to count by 5s**.

On Your Own
Solve.

Look at the pattern. Write the missing numbers. Write a rule.

22   ___   26   28   ___   32

Rule: Count by _____

All-Star Math 1–2, SV 9781419099205

Name _____ Date _____

Practice
Solve.

1. Look at the pattern. Write the missing numbers. Write a rule.

67   68   ___   70   ___   72

Rule: Count by _____

2. Look at the pattern. Write the missing numbers. Write a rule.

0   10   ___   30   40   ___

Rule: Count by _____

3. Look at the pattern. Write the missing numbers. Write a rule.

12   15   18   ___   ___   27

Rule: Count by _____

Name _____   Date _____

Lesson Greater Than and Less Than

Count the number of each group of football helmets below.
Write each number. Find the group of helmets that is greater.
Circle **>** or **<** .

_____   **>** **<**   _____

Think About It

• Read the problem.

• What are you looking for?

  the greater group of football helmets

• What data do you have to help you solve the problem?

  4 football helmets and 2 football helmets

• Think about the information you have.

  I know there are 4 football helmets and 2 football helmets.
  First I write those numbers. Then I need to find out which
  number is greater. I know that > means "greater than" and
  < means "less than." I pick the symbol that tells whether 4 is
  greater than or less than 2.

• Solve the problem.

  Since **4 is greater than 2**, I circle **>** .

On Your Own
Solve.

Count the number of bobsleds. Write each number. Circle **>** or **<** .

_____   **>** **<**   _____

Name _____ Date _____

Practice
Solve.

1. Count the number of basketball goals. Write each number.
   Circle > or < .

   _____ > < _____

2. Count the number of swim goggles. Write each number.
   Circle > or < .

   _____ > < _____

3. Count the number of whistles. Write each number. Circle > or < .

   _____ > < _____

4. Count the number of baseball bats. Write each number.
   Circle > or < .

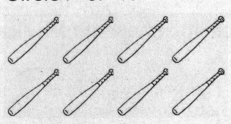 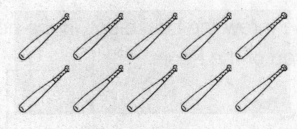

   _____ > < _____

All-Star Math 1–2, SV 9781419099205

Name _____   Date _____

Lesson 20   Identifying Shapes

Evan threw the baseball. Circle the shape that is like a baseball.

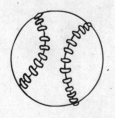 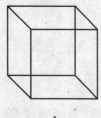 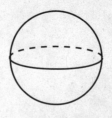 

cube   sphere   cone

Think About It
- Read the problem.
- What are you looking for?
  the **shape** that is **like a baseball**
- What data do you have to help you solve the problem?
  three shapes: a cube, sphere, and cone
- Think about the information you have.
  I know that a baseball is round. I need to find the picture of the shape that is round like a baseball. I look at the cube, sphere, and cone.
- Solve the problem.
  The sphere is like a baseball. So I circle the **sphere**.

On Your Own
Solve.

Maria threw the basketball in the hoop. Circle the shape that is like the top of the hoop.

   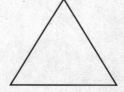 

All-Star Math 1–2, SV 9781419099205

Name _____ Date _____

Practice
Solve.

1. Avon marked the playing field. Circle the shape that is like the things he used to mark the field.

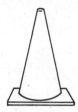

                    sphere   cone   cylinder

2. Tyrone took his new hockey puck out of the box. Circle the shape that is like the box.

   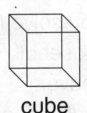      

                    cube   cone   cylinder

3. The teacher asked Sue to put all the balls in the basket. Circle the shape that is like the basket.

      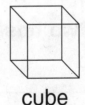   

                    sphere   cube   cylinder

4. Tami and her friends wanted to play baseball. Tami drew a shape in the dirt to show where the bases were. Circle the shape that is like what Tami drew.

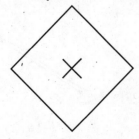   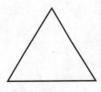   

Unit 5: Geometry and Patterns
All-Star Math 1–2, SV 9781419099205

Name _____ Date _____

Lesson Congruent Figures

Circle the balls that are the same shape and size.

Think About It
- Read the problem.
- What are you looking for?
   the **balls** that are the **same shape and size**
- What data do you have to help you solve the problem?
   baseball, football, basketball, baseball, and golf ball
- Think about the information you have.
   I look at the different kinds of balls. The football is not round.
   The basketball is too big. The golf ball is too small. The
   baseballs are the same shape and size.
- Solve the problem.
   So I circle the **two baseballs** because they are the same
   shape and size.

On Your Own
Solve.

Circle the sports gear that are the same shape and size.

Name _____ Date _____

Practice
Solve.

1. Circle the shoes that are the same shape and size.

2. Circle the headgear that are the same shape and size.

    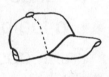

3. Circle the skis that are the same shape and size.

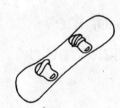 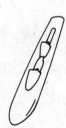 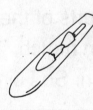 

4. Circle the ribbons that are the same shape and size.

Lesson 22   Symmetry

Circle the two parts that do **NOT** match.

Think About It

- Read the problem.
- What are you looking for?
  the **two parts** that **do NOT match**
- What data do you have to help you solve the problem?
  a football, bowling pin, and a hockey stick with dashed lines
- Think about the information you have.
  I look at the football, the bowling pin, and the hockey stick. I
  think about what each object would look like if I cut the
  picture along the line. Would the two parts match?
- Solve the problem.
  The two parts of the football match. The two parts of the
  bowling pin match. The two parts of the hockey stick would
  NOT match. So I circle **the hockey stick**.

On Your Own
Solve.

Circle the two parts
that do **NOT** match.

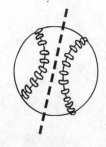      

Name _____ Date _____

Practice
Solve.

1. Circle the two parts that do **NOT** match.

 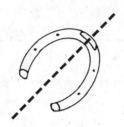 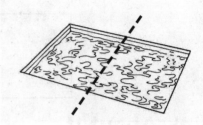

2. Circle the two parts that do **NOT** match.

 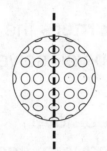 

3. Circle the two parts that do **NOT** match.

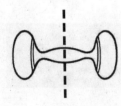 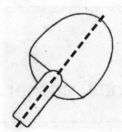 

4. Circle the two parts that do **NOT** match.

 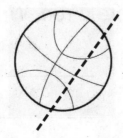 

Name _____ Date _____

Lesson 23 Sides and Corners

Coach Pérez bought some new bases for the baseball field.
Write how many sides and corners one base has.

_____ sides

_____ corners

Think About It

- Read the problem.
- What are you looking for?
  the number of **sides** and **corners** the base has
- What data do you have to help you solve the problem?
  a square base
- Think about the information you have.
  I know that this shape is a square. I count 4 sides. I also
  count 4 corners.
- Solve the problem.
  4 sides
  4 corners
  So the base has **4 sides** and **4 corners**.

On Your Own
Solve.

Devon slid into home plate to score a run. Write how many sides and
corners the home plate has.

_____ sides

_____ corners

Name _____ Date _____

Practice
Solve.

1. Karla had a pennant for her favorite football team. Write how many sides and corners the pennant has.

_____ sides

_____ corners

2. Pedro waved the flag as the race cars crossed the finish line. Write how many sides and corners the flag has.

_____ sides

_____ corners

3. The bike wheel is shaped like a circle. Write how many sides and corners the wheel has.

_____ sides

_____ corners

4. A baseball field is shaped like a diamond. Write how many sides and corners it has.

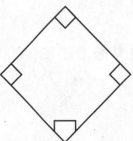

_____ sides

_____ corners

Lesson ⭐24 Extending a Pattern

Look at the pattern of balls.

Which ball will come next? Circle it.

Think About It

• Read the problem.

• What are you looking for?
  the **ball** that comes **next in the pattern**

• What data do you have to help you solve the problem?
  4 footballs and 2 baseballs in a line

• Think about the information you have.
  I know that there are 2 footballs, then 2 baseballs, and then 2
  more footballs. I should think about the pattern and decide
  which ball will come next in line.

• Solve the problem.
  The last time there were 2 footballs, a baseball was next. Now
  I know that after the next 2 footballs, there should be a
  baseball. So I circle the picture of the **baseball**.

On Your Own
Solve.

Look at the pattern.

Which picture will come next? Circle it.

Name _____   Date _____

Practice
Solve.

1. Look at the pattern. Which picture will come next? Circle it.

2. Look at the pattern. Which picture will come next? Circle it.

 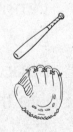

3. Look at the pattern. Which picture will come next? Circle it.

4. Look at the pattern. Which picture will come next? Circle it.

Name _____ Date _____

Lesson ⭐25 Length, Weight, and Volume

The boxer stepped into the ring. About how much does the boxer weigh? Circle the best answer.

200 ounces   200 pounds

Think About It
- Read the problem.
- What are you looking for?
  about how much the boxer **weighs**
- What data do you have to help you solve the problem?
  a boxer
  200 ounces
  200 pounds
- Think about the information you have.
  I know that ounces are used to measure smaller things like baby birds. Pounds are used to measure larger things like people. I know that a boxer is a person.
- Solve the problem.
  So I circle **200 pounds**.

On Your Own
Solve.

Candy's team played on the new football field. How long is a football field? Circle the best answer.

120 yards   120 inches

Name _____ Date _____

Practice
Solve.

1. Jarrod weighed his new baseball. About how much did the baseball weigh? Circle the best answer.

    5 ounces   5 pounds

2. Michelle scored by throwing the basketball in the hoop. How high was the basket? Circle the best answer.

    10 feet   10 miles

3. David won the race in the swimming pool. About how much water was in the pool? Circle the best answer.

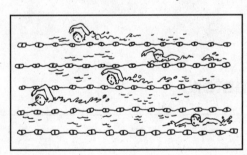

    31,000 ounces   31,000 gallons

4. During an ice hockey game, Jermaine hit the puck into the goal. About how thick is the puck? Circle the best answer.

    1 yard   1 inch

Lesson 26   Perimeter

Van measured the sides of the swimming pool. The perimeter is the distance around the pool. What is the perimeter of the pool?

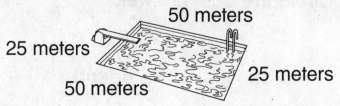

Think About It
- Read the problem.
- What are you looking for?
  the **perimeter** of the **pool**
- What data do you have to help you solve the problem?
  The sides measure 50, 25, 50, and 25.
- Think about the information you have.
  I know that Van measured the sides of the pool. I know that the perimeter is the distance around the pool. If I add the sides, I will find the perimeter.
- Solve the problem.
  $$50 + 25 + 50 + 25 = 150$$
  So the perimeter of the pool is **150 meters**.

On Your Own
Solve.

The picture shows a field used for field hockey.
What is the perimeter of the field?

100 yds

60 yds   60 yds

100 yds

Name _____ Date _____

Practice

Solve.

1. Mr. Zavala bought new bases to put on the baseball field at the school. Each base measures 14 inches on each side. What is the perimeter of one base?

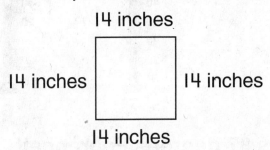

14 inches

14 inches   14 inches

14 inches

2. Cal and his dad built a boxing ring. What is the perimeter of the boxing ring?

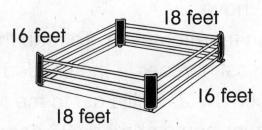

18 feet

16 feet

16 feet

18 feet

3. Anna runs around a field each day after school. What is the perimeter of the field?

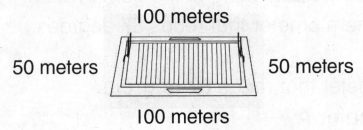

100 meters

50 meters   50 meters

100 meters

4. Ken bought a new golf flag. What is the perimeter of the flag?

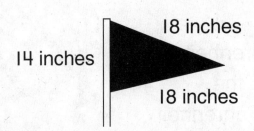

18 inches

14 inches

18 inches

Name _____   Date _____

Lesson 27   Temperature

The temperature was 87 degrees
Fahrenheit when the volleyball game
started. Circle the thermometer that
shows 87 degrees Fahrenheit.

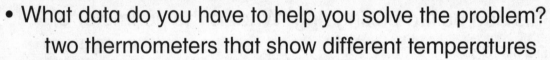

Think About It

• Read the problem.
• What are you looking for?

    the **thermometer** that shows **87 degrees Fahrenheit**

• What data do you have to help you solve the problem?

    two thermometers that show different temperatures

• Think about the information you have.

    I know that I need to read both thermometers. To read the first
    thermometer, I look at the closest number to the shaded area.
    That is 80 degrees. Then I count by 2s until I get to the top of
    the shaded area. I know this thermometer reads 87 degrees.
    Now I look at the second thermometer. It reads 37 degrees.
    Since the temperature at the beginning of the game was
    87 degrees, I find the thermometer that reads 87 degrees.

• Solve the problem.

    So I circle the thermometer that reads **87 degrees
    Fahrenheit, Thermometer A**.

On Your Own
Solve.

The temperature was 32 degrees Fahrenheit
when the bobsled races began. Circle the
thermometer that shows 32 degrees Fahrenheit.

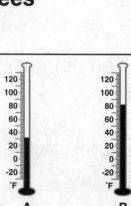

Unit 6: Measurement and Fractions
All-Star Math 1–2, SV 9781419099205

Practice
Solve.

1. The temperature was 68° Fahrenheit when Track-and-Field Day started. Circle the thermometer that shows 68° Fahrenheit.

2. The temperature was 95° Fahrenheit when the swim meet started. Circle the thermometer that shows 95° Fahrenheit.

3. The temperature was 72° Fahrenheit when the horse race started. Circle the thermometer that shows 72° Fahrenheit.

4. The temperature was 46° Fahrenheit when the football game started. Circle the thermometer that shows 46° Fahrenheit.

Name _____   Date _____

Miles played in $\frac{1}{2}$ of the football game. Circle the shape that shows the fraction for $\frac{1}{2}$.

Think About It

- Read the problem.
- What are you looking for?
  the shape that shows the **fraction for $\frac{1}{2}$**
- What data do you have to help you solve the problem?
  Miles played in $\frac{1}{2}$ of the game.
  circle with 1 of 2 parts shaded
  circle with 1 of 4 parts shaded
- Think about the information you have.
  I know that Miles played in $\frac{1}{2}$ of the football game. The fraction $\frac{1}{2}$ will have two equal pieces. One of the pieces will be shaded. I look for the fraction that has 1 out of 2 pieces shaded.
- Solve the problem.
  So I circle the shape that shows the fraction for $\frac{1}{2}$.

On Your Own
Solve.

Maria was in first place for $\frac{1}{3}$ of the race. Circle the shape that shows the fraction for $\frac{1}{3}$.

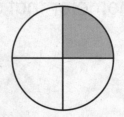
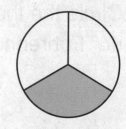

Name _____ Date _____

Practice

Solve.

1. When it rained at the football game, $\frac{4}{6}$ of the fans got wet. Circle the shape that shows the fraction for $\frac{4}{6}$.

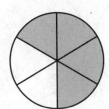 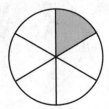

2. The first grade students ran $\frac{3}{4}$ mile to finish the race. Circle the shape that shows the fraction for $\frac{3}{4}$.

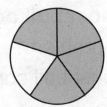 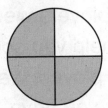

3. The second grade students sold $\frac{4}{5}$ of the tickets for the softball game. Circle the shape that shows the fraction for $\frac{4}{5}$.

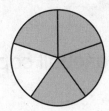 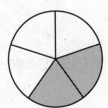

4. At a store, $\frac{2}{3}$ of the bats were made from wood. Circle the shape that shows the fraction for $\frac{2}{3}$.

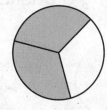 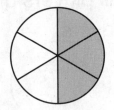

Unit 6: Measurement and Fractions
All-Star Math 1–2, SV 9781419099205

Name _____ Date _____

Lesson 29 Parts of a Group

How many baseball players are wearing baseball caps? Circle the correct fraction of all the baseball players.

$\frac{1}{3}$ $\frac{1}{2}$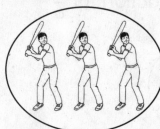

Think About It

• Read the problem.

• What are you looking for?

  the **fraction** of baseball players **wearing baseball caps**

• What data do you have to help you solve the problem?

  9 baseball players and 3 players wearing baseball caps

• Think about the information you have.

  I know that 3 out of the 9 players are wearing baseball caps.

  I write a fraction that shows the part of the group that is wearing baseball caps.

• Solve the problem.

  Since 1 group out of 3 groups is wearing baseball caps, the fraction is $\frac{1}{3}$.

On Your Own
Solve.

How many groups of basketball players are holding a basketball? Circle the correct fraction of players.

$\frac{1}{4}$ $\frac{1}{6}$

Unit 6: Measurement and Fractions
All-Star Math 1–2, SV 9781419099205

Name _____ Date _____

Practice
Solve.

1. How many football players are wearing helmets? Circle the correct fraction of players.

$\frac{1}{3}$ $\frac{1}{2}$ 

2. How many targets have an arrow? Circle the correct fraction of targets.

$\frac{1}{3}$ $\frac{2}{3}$ 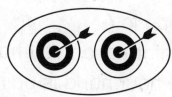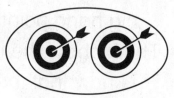

3. How many runners are holding torches? Circle the correct fraction of runners.

$\frac{3}{4}$ $\frac{1}{4}$ 

4. How many fishing rods have a fish? Circle the correct fraction of rods.

$\frac{3}{5}$ $\frac{2}{5}$ 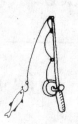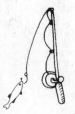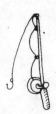

Unit 6: Measurement and Fractions
All-Star Math 1–2, SV 9781419099205

Name _____   Date _____

Lesson 30 Reading a Clock

The clock shows the time the swim meet starts.

What time does the clock show? _____

Think About It

• Read the problem.

• What are you looking for?

   the time that the clock shows

• What data do you have to help you solve the problem?

   a clock with the little hand pointing between 9 and 10 and the
   big hand pointing to 6

• Think about the information you have.

   I know that the hour hand is pointing between 9 and 10. That
   tells me that the time is after 9:00. I know that the minute
   hand is pointing to 6. I need to find how many minutes after 9
   it is. I count by 5s from the 12 to the 6.

• Solve the problem.

   It is 30 minutes after 9:00.

   So that means the swim meet starts at **9:30**.

On Your Own
Solve.

The clock shows the time the ice-skating race

ended. What time does the clock show? _____

Name _____ Date _____

Practice
Solve.

1. The clock shows the time a football game started. What time does the clock show? _____

2. Neal set the clock to let people know the time the tennis match will start. What time does the clock show? _____

3. Pete looked at his watch to see the time he finished the bike race. What time did his watch show? _____

4. Kate was late to her karate class. The clock shows the time she got to class. What does the clock show? _____

Name _____ Date _____

Lesson Reading a Calendar

June						
Sunday	**Monday**	**Tuesday**	**Wednesday**	**Thursday**	**Friday**	**Saturday**
6	7	8	9	10	11	12
	swim laps	swim laps			swim meet	Grandma's house

Look at the calendar. On which date did Kasey have a swim meet?

_____

Think About It

- Read the problem.
- What are you looking for?

    the **date of** Kasey's **swim meet**

- What data do you have to help you solve the problem?

    7 and 8 = swim laps, 11 = swim meet, 12 = Grandma's house

- Think about the information you have.

    I know that the calendar shows <u>swim meet</u> by the number <u>11</u>.

    The calendar is for the month of June.

- Solve the problem.

    So the swim meet is on **June 11**.

On Your Own
Solve.

Look at the calendar above. On which dates did Kasey swim laps?

June _____

All-Star Math 1–2, SV 9781419099205

Name _____   Date _____

Practice
Solve.

June						
Sunday	**Monday**	**Tuesday**	**Wednesday**	**Thursday**	**Friday**	**Saturday**
					1	2 bike races
3	4	5 baseball practice	6	7	8 baseball game	9
10	11	12	13 baseball practice	14	15 baseball game	16
17	18	19 baseball practice	20	21	22	23 baseball game
24	25 baseball practice	26	27	28	29 baseball game	30 baseball team picnic

This is a page from Javier's calendar. Look at the calendar. Then answer the questions.

1. On which date did Javier's baseball team have a picnic?

June _____

2. On which dates did Javier have baseball practice?

June _____

3. On which dates did Javier have a baseball game?

June _____

4. On which date did Javier go to the bike races?

June _____

Unit 7: Time and Money
All-Star Math 1–2, SV 9781419099205

Lesson 32 Counting Money

Color the coins that you need to buy the baseball cap.

Think About It

- Read the problem.
- What are you looking for?

  the **coins** that I need **to buy the baseball cap**
- What data do you have to help you solve the problem?

  baseball cap = 95¢; 3 quarters, 3 dimes, and 3 pennies.
- Think about the information you have.

  I know the baseball cap costs 95¢. The quarters are worth 25¢ each, the dimes are worth 10¢ each, and the pennies are worth 1¢ each. I look at which coins will add up to 95¢.
- Solve the problem.

  25¢ + 25¢ + 25¢ + 10¢ + 10¢ = 95¢

  So I color **3 quarters** and **2 dimes** because they add up to **95¢**.

On Your Own
Solve.

Color the coins that you need to buy the tennis ball.

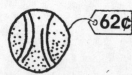 

Name _____ Date _____

Practice
Solve.

1. Color the coins that you need to buy the paddle.

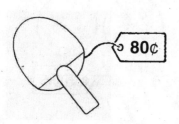  

2. Color the coins that you need to buy the horseshoe.

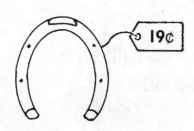  

3. Color the coins that you need to buy the baseball.

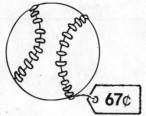   

4. Color the coins that you need to buy a ticket to the football game.

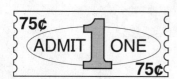  

Unit 7: Time and Money
All-Star Math 1–2, SV 9781419099205

Name _____   Date _____

Lesson 33   Equal Amounts

Show a different way to make the same amount. Draw the coins you would use. Write the value on each coin.

50¢

Think About It

- Read the problem.
- What are you looking for?

  a **different way** to make the **same amount**

- What data do you have to help you solve the problem?

  2 quarters; fishhook = 50¢

- Think about the information you have.

  I know the fishhook costs 50¢. I can make 50¢ with two quarters. I think about other coins that make 50¢.

- Solve the problem.

  So there are many ways to make 50¢. I could use **5 dimes OR 10 nickels OR 50 pennies**. I could also use different coins, like **3 dimes and 4 nickels**.

On Your Own
Solve.

Show a different way to make the same amount. Draw the coins you would use. Write the value on each coin.

19¢

Name _____   Date _____

Practice

Solve. Show a different way to make the same amount. Draw the
coins you would use. Write the value on each coin.

1.

2.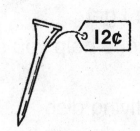

3.

4.

Unit 7: Time and Money
All-Star Math 1–2, SV 9781419099205

Name _____   Date _____

Lesson Counting Change

You have $1.00 to spend. Count up from the price of the flying disc to find how much change you should get back.

_____   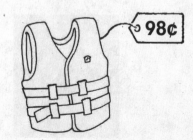 75¢

Think About It

- Read the problem.
- What are you looking for?
  how much change I get
- What data do you have to help you solve the problem?
  $1.00 to spend
  $0.75 = cost of the flying disc
- Think about the information you have.
  I know that I have $1.00 to spend. I know the flying disc costs $0.75. I count up from $0.75 to $1.00 to find out how much change I will get.
- Solve the problem.
  I can count by 5s from 75¢ to 1 dollar: 75¢, 80¢, 85¢, 90¢, 95¢, $1.00.
  So I know I will get **$0.25 back** when I buy the flying disc.

On Your Own
Solve.

I have $1.00 to spend. I count up from the price to find how much change I get back.

_____   98¢

All-Star Math 1–2, SV 9781419099205

Name _____ Date _____

Practice
Solve.

1. You have $1.00 to spend. Count up from the price to find how much change you should get back.

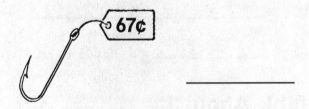

_____

2. You have $1.00 to spend. Count up from the price to find how much change you should get back.

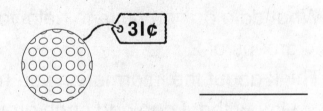

_____

3. You have $1.00 to spend. Count up from the price to find how much change you should get back.

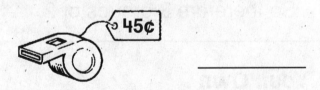

_____

4. You have $1.00 to spend. Count up from the price to find how much change you should get back.

_____

Lesson Adding Equal Groups

Write the addition sentence. Then write how many groups of 2.

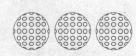

_____ + _____ + _____ = _____

_____ groups of 2

Think About It

- Read the problem.
- What are you looking for?
  addition sentence and how many **groups of 2**
- What data do you have to help you solve the problem?
  groups of 2
- Think about the information you have.
  I know that I can add each group of 2 to get the addition
  sentence. I will add 2 + 2 + 2. I am adding 3 groups.
- Solve the problem.
  2 + 2 + 2 = 6
  So there are **3** groups of 2.

On Your Own
Solve.

Write the addition sentence. Then write how many groups of 3.

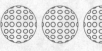

_____ + _____ + _____ + _____ = _____

_____ groups of 3

All-Star Math 1–2, SV 9781419099205

Name _____ Date _____

Practice
Solve.

1. Write the addition sentence. Then write how many groups of 3.

_____ + _____ + _____ = _____

_____ groups of 3

2. Write the addition sentence. Then write how many groups of 2.

_____ + _____ = _____

_____ groups of 2

3. Write the addition sentence. Then write how many groups of 2.

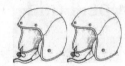  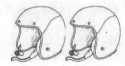 

_____ + _____ + _____ + _____ = _____

_____ groups of 2

4. Write the addition sentence. Then write how many groups of 6.

_____ + _____ + _____ = _____

_____ groups of 6

Unit 8: Multiplication and Division
All-Star Math 1–2, SV 9781419099205

Name _____ Date _____

Lesson 36   Exploring Multiplication

Circle groups of 2 to find the total. Complete the sentences.

_____ + _____ + _____ + _____ + _____ = _____

_____ groups of 2

_____ × 2 = _____

Think About It

- Read the problem.
- What are you looking for?
  how many **tennis shoes**
- What data do you have to help you solve the problem?
  2 tennis shoes in each group and 5 groups
- Think about the information you have.
  I know that when I circle groups of 2, I have 5 groups. I add
  5 groups of 2. I multiply 5 groups of 2.
- Solve the problem.
  2 + 2 + 2 + 2 + 2 = 10, 5 groups of 2 = 10, 5 × 2 = 10
  So there are **10 tennis shoes**.

On Your Own
Solve.

Circle groups of 3 to find the total. Complete the sentences.

a. _____ + _____ + _____ + _____ = _____

b. _____ groups of 3

c. _____ × 3 = _____

All-Star Math 1–2, SV 9781419099205

Practice
Solve.

1. Circle groups of 4 to find the total. Complete the sentences.

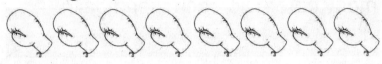

a. _____ + _____ = _____

b. _____ groups of 4

c. _____ × 4 = _____

2. Circle groups of 3 to find the total. Complete the sentences.

a. _____ + _____ + _____ = _____

b. _____ groups of 3

c. _____ × 3 = _____

3. Circle groups of 2 to find the total. Complete the sentences.

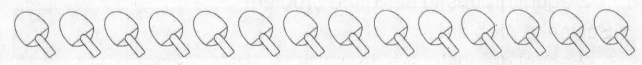

a. ____ + ____ + ____ + ____ + ____ + ____ + ____ = ____

b. ____ groups of 2

c. ____ × 2 = ____

4. Circle groups of 3 to find the total. Complete the sentences.

a. ____ + ____ + ____ + ____ + ____ + ____ = ____

b. ____ groups of 3

c. ____ × 3 = ____

Name _____ Date _____

Lesson Understanding Division

Steve had 16 baseball cards. He gave an equal number of cards to each of 2 friends. How many cards did each friend get?

Think About It

• Read the problem.

• What are you looking for?

  the number of **baseball cards** Steve **gave to each friend**

• What data do you have to help you solve the problem?

  16 baseball cards and 2 friends

• Think about the information you have.

  I know Steve had 16 baseball cards. He gave the same
  number of cards to 2 friends. I divide the 16 cards into
  2 equal groups to solve the problem.

• Solve the problem.

  2 equal groups of 8 = 16

  So Steve **gave each friend 8 baseball cards**.

On Your Own
Solve.

Lela found 16 golf balls in a field. She put the balls in 4 equal groups. How many balls were in each group? _____

Name _____ Date _____

Practice
Solve.

1. There were 8 racehorses in the barn. The owner put an equal number of horses in each of 2 pastures. How many horses were in each pasture? _____

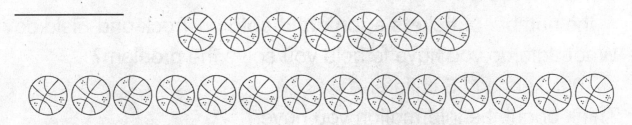

2. The coach had 21 basketballs. He put an equal number on each of 3 shelves. How many balls were on each shelf? _____

3. Jenny shot 16 arrows. An equal number of arrows went into each of 2 targets. How many arrows are in each target?

_____

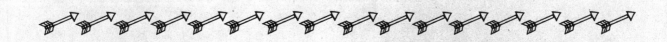

4. Neal has an equal number of weight on the 2 ends of a dumbbell. He has a total of 20 pounds on the dumbbell. How many pounds are on each end of the dumbbell? _____

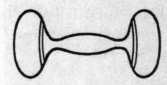

Name _____   Date _____

Lesson Practicing Division

Chloe, Jim, Andy, Greg, and Alvin had 10 tickets to sell for their
school's Track-and-Field day. Each child sold an equal number of
tickets. How many tickets did each child sell? Complete the
division sentence.

10 ÷ 5 = _____

Think About It
- Read the problem.
- What are you looking for?
    the number of **tickets each child sold** on Track-and-Field day
- What data do you have to help you solve the problem?
    10 tickets and 5 children
- Think about the information you have.
    I know there are 5 children selling 10 tickets. I also know that
    each child sold the same number of tickets. I need to find how
    many tickets each child sold. I divide to solve the problem.
- Solve the problem.
    10 ÷ 5 = 2
    So each child sold **2 tickets**.

On Your Own
Solve.

Tyra had 9 tennis balls. She put them in tubes that held 3 balls each.
How many tubes did Tyra use? Complete the division sentence.

9 ÷ 3 = _____

Name _____ Date _____

Practice
Solve.

1. There were 12 judges for a gymnastics contest. The judges were put in groups of 4. How many groups of judges were there? Complete the division sentence.

$$12 \div 4 = \underline{\hspace{2cm}}$$

2. There were 14 players on a handball court. The players were equally divided into 2 teams. How many players were on each team? Complete the division sentence.

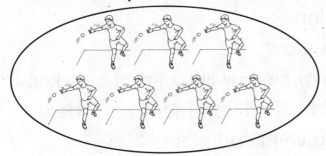 

$$14 \div 2 = \underline{\hspace{2cm}}$$

3. Last summer, 18 students signed up to play baseball. Each team had 9 players. How many teams were there? Complete the division sentence.

$$18 \div 9 = \underline{\hspace{2cm}}$$

All-Star Math 1–2, SV 9781419099205

Name _____ Date _____

Lesson 39   Choose the Operation

Sunny and her friends use 2 lanes at a bowling alley. There are 10 pins in each lane. How many pins are there altogether?

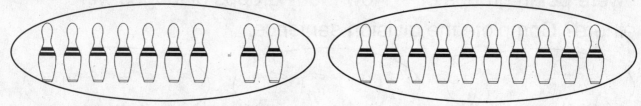

Think About It

• Read the problem.

• What are you looking for?

   the number of **pins** there are **altogether**

• What data do you have to help you solve the problem?

   2 lanes and 10 pins in each lane

• Think about the information you have.

   I know that 2 lanes are used at the bowling alley. I also know each lane has 10 pins. I need to find how many pins there are altogether. I multiply to solve the problem.

• Solve the problem.

   10 pins × 2 lanes = 20 pins

   So there are **20 pins** in the bowling alley lanes.

On Your Own
Solve.

There are 12 volleyballs in a store. Each shelf has 6 volleyballs on it. How many shelves of volleyballs are there?

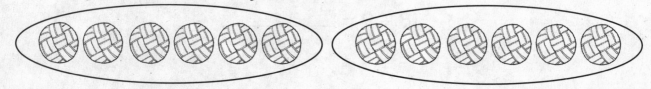

Unit 8: Multiplication and Division
All-Star Math 1–2, SV 9781419099205

Name _____   Date _____

Practice
Solve.

1. A man went to practice hitting golf balls. He hit 3 balls in 3 minutes. How many balls did the man hit?

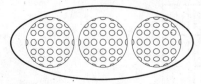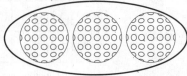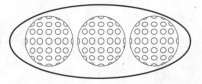

2. A store has 12 footballs. The clerk puts an equal number of footballs on each of 3 shelves. How many footballs are on each shelf?

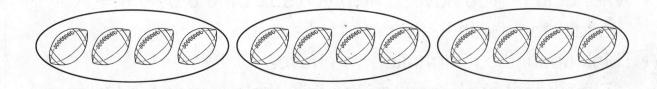

3. There are 6 lanes on a track. Each lane has 1 runner on it. How many runners are there?

4. There were 5 softball teams. The coach gave 2 softballs to each team. How many softballs did the coach give to the teams?

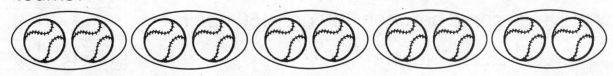

Unit 8: Multiplication and Division
All-Star Math 1–2, SV 9781419099205

Name _____   Date _____

Lesson Tally Tables

A group of friends went bowling. They used a tally table to show the players' scores. How many players scored between 120 and 130 points?

120-130	II
130-140	IIII
140-150	III
150-160	I

_____ players

Think About It

• Read the problem.

• What are you looking for?

 How many **players** scored **between 120** and **130** points

• What data do you have to help you solve the problem?

 a tally table with 4 groups of tallies

• Think about the information you have.

 I know that each mark on the tally table stands for 1 player. I look for the scores 120–130. I count the tally marks next to 120–130.

• Solve the problem.

 There are 2 tally marks next to 120–130, so that means there were **2 players** who scored between 120 and 130 points.

On Your Own
Solve.

The next week, the friends went bowling again. They used a new tally table to show the players' scores. How many players scored between 140 and 150 points?

120-130	III
130-140	IIII
140-150	III
150-160	II

_____ players

Name _____ Date _____

Practice
Solve.

The tally table shows how many points 4 friends scored in 3 games.
Use the tally table to answer the questions.

	Kareem	Delia	Ling	Stacy
Game 1	卌 //	//	卌	/
Game 2	卌	卌	卌	卌
Game 3	卌 卌	卌	/	///

I. Who scored the fewest points in Game I?   _____

How many points did that player score?   _____

2. How many points did each player score in Game 2?

Kareem: _____

Delia: _____

Ling: _____

Stacy: _____

3. In Game 3, how many more points did Stacy score than Ling?

_____

4. Who scored the most points in Game 3?   _____

How many points did that player score?   _____

Name _____   Date _____

Lesson Picture Graphs

Look at the graph. How many times did Van throw the football?

Number of Throws					
Van	🏈	🏈	🏈	🏈	🏈
Tina	🏈	🏈	🏈		

Key: 🏈 = 2 throws

_____ times

Think About It

• Read the problem.
• What are you looking for?
  the number of **times Van threw the football**
• What data do you have to help you solve the problem?
  5 pictures of footballs next to Van's name
• Think about the information you have.

  I know to look at the key first. It tells me that each picture stands for 2 throws. Next I count the pictures next to Van's name. I need to find how many throws the 5 pictures of footballs stand for. I count by 2s to solve the problem.
• Solve the problem.

  $2 + 2 + 2 + 2 + 2 = 10$

  So Van threw the football **10 times**.

On Your Own
Solve.

Look at the graph. How many arrows did Kate shoot into the target?

Arrows Shot in Target							
Taylor	➵	➵	➵	➵	➵	➵	
Kate	➵	➵	➵	➵	➵	➵	➵

Key: ➵ = 1 arrow

_____ arrows

Name _____ Date _____

Practice
Solve.

Use the graph to answer the questions.

Manuel's Baseball Card Collection

Year	Number of Cards Collected
1994	☐ ☐ ☐ ☐ ☐
1995	☐ ☐ ☐ ☐ ☐ ☐ ☐ ☐
1996	☐ ☐ ☐ ☐ ☐ ☐ ☐ ☐ ☐
1997	☐ ☐ ☐ ☐ ☐ ☐ ☐ ☐
1998	☐

Key: ☐ = 5 cards

1. In which year did Manuel collect the most baseball cards?

_____

2. How many baseball cards did Manuel collect each year?

1994: _____

1995: _____

1996: _____

1997: _____

1998: _____

3. How many more baseball cards did Manuel collect in 1996 than 1995? _____

4. How many more baseball cards did Manuel collect in 1994 than 1998? _____

Name _____   Date _____

Lesson 42   Bar Graphs

Look at the graph. How many home runs did Pablo hit?

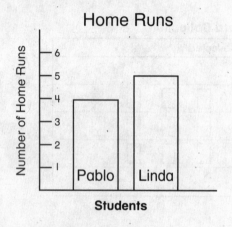

_____ home runs

Think About It

- Read the problem.
- What are you looking for?

  the number of **home runs** Pablo **hit**

- What data do you have to help you solve the problem?

  a bar graph showing the home runs Linda and Pablo hit

- Think about the information you have.

  I know to look for the bar above Pablo's name. When I find the top of the bar, I look across to the left to see what number is there. I see the number 4.

- Solve the problem.

  Since Pablo's bar goes to 4 on the graph, I know he hit **4 home runs**.

On Your Own
Solve.

Look at the graph above. How many home runs did Linda hit?

_____ home runs

Name _____ Date _____

Practice
Solve.

Use the graph to answer the questions.

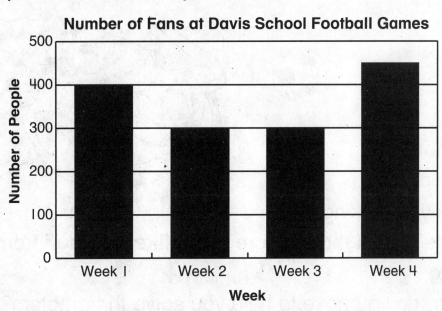

Number of Fans at Davis School Football Games

1. How many people came to see the games each week?

   Week 1: _____

   Week 2: _____

   Week 3: _____

   Week 4: _____

2. In which week did the most people come to the games?

   _____

3. In which two weeks did about the same number of people
   come to the games? _____

4. About what is the total number of people that came to the
   games during the 4 weeks? _____

All-Star Math 1–2, SV 9781419099205

Lesson Understanding Probability

Which type of ball are you most likely to pull from the bag?
Circle your answer.

Think About It

- Read the problem.
- What are you looking for?

  the type of **ball** that you are **most likely to pull** from
  the bag

- What data do you have to help you solve the problem?

  5 footballs, 4 basketballs, and 3 baseballs

- Think about the information you have.

  I know to count the number of each ball in the bag. I look
  for which type of ball has the largest number to find out
  which one I will most likely pull.

- Solve the problem.

  Since there are more footballs, I will **most likely pull out
  a football**.

Name _____ Date _____

Practice
Solve.

1. Which type of ball are you most likely to pull from the bag? Circle your answer.

2. Which type of ball are you least likely to pull from the bag? Circle your answer.

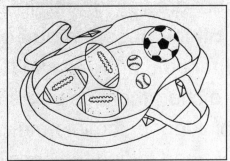

3. Which type of ball are you most likely to pull from the bag? Circle your answer.

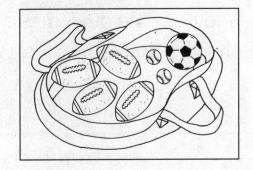

4. Which type of ball are you least likely to pull from the bag? Circle your answer.

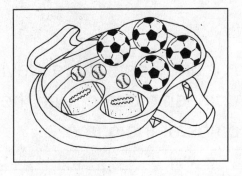

Unit 9: Data and Analysis
All-Star Math 1–2, SV 9781419099205

Name _____   Date _____

Lesson 44 Possible Outcomes

Pete and Lula ran a race. In what order could they finish? Use the chart to write all the possible outcomes of the race.

First	Second

Think About It

- Read the problem.
- What are you looking for?

    all the **possible outcomes** of the race

- What data do you have to help you solve the problem?

    a chart that has boxes for first and second place

- Think about the information you have.

    I need to find the possible outcomes of the race. I use the chart to list the names in different orders until I have found all the possible outcomes.

- Solve the problem.

First	Second
Pete	Lula
Lula	Pete

On Your Own
Solve.

Team 1 and Team 2 are playing against each other in the championship game. Use the chart to write all the possible outcomes of the game.

Win	Lose

Practice
Solve.

1. Today Rosa will play football and baseball with her friends. They will play 1 sport in the morning and 1 sport in the afternoon. Use the chart to write all the possible outcomes.

Morning	Afternoon

2. Dean and Sara had an ice-skating race. In what order could they finish the race? Use the chart to write all the possible outcomes of the race.

First	Second

3. Martina has math and reading homework. She can do her homework in any order. Use the chart to write all the possible outcomes.

First	Second

4. Team 1, Team 2, and Team 3 are playing in a tennis tournament. Use the chart to write all the possible outcomes of the tournament.

First	Second	Third

⭐ Answer Key

Unit 1

page 6
On Your Own: 5 players should be colored.

page 7
1. 6 players should be colored.
2. 3 arrows should be colored.
3. 4 paddles should be colored.
4. 10 pins should be colored.

page 8
On Your Own: 4, 9; 9 should be circled.

page 9
1. 5, 3; 3 should be circled.
2. 6, 8; 8 should be circled.
3. 2, 6; 2 should be circled.
4. 4, 1; 4 should be circled.

page 10
On Your Own: There should be a line drawn between 10 — ten; 9 — nine; and 8 — eight.

page 11
There should be a line drawn between 1 — one; 6 — six; 3 — three; 7 — seven; 5 — five; 2 — two; 4 — four; and 8 — eight.

page 12
On Your Own: 10 should be written.

page 13
Numbers should be written in this order: 2, 3, 4, 5, 6, 7, 8, 9.

page 14
On Your Own: The third swimmer from the finish line should be circled.

page 15
1. The second car from the finish line should be circled.
2. The fifth batter behind home plate should be circled.
3. The fourth jumper behind the line should be circled.
4. The first child at the ticket counter should be circled.

Unit 2

page 16
On Your Own: 7 points

page 17
1. 3 fish
2. 5 times
3. 7 ribbons
4. 5 times

page 18
On Your Own: 5 + 7 = 12

page 19
1. 2 + 4 = 6
2. 8 + 1 = 9
3. 9 + 3 = 12
4. 4 + 4 = 8

page 20
On Your Own:
$$\begin{array}{r} 2 \\ +\ 4 \\ \hline 6 \end{array}$$

page 21
1.
$$\begin{array}{r} 3 \\ +\ 2 \\ \hline 5 \end{array}$$
2.
$$\begin{array}{r} 6 \\ +\ 3 \\ \hline 9 \end{array}$$
3.
$$\begin{array}{r} 5 \\ +\ 5 \\ \hline 10 \end{array}$$
4.
$$\begin{array}{r} 5 \\ +\ 3 \\ \hline 8 \end{array}$$

page 22
On Your Own:
$$\begin{array}{r} 4 \\ 2 \\ +\ 2 \\ \hline 8 \end{array}$$

page 23
1.
$$\begin{array}{r} 3 \\ 4 \\ +\ 3 \\ \hline 10 \end{array}$$
2.
$$\begin{array}{r} 2 \\ 3 \\ +\ 3 \\ \hline 8 \end{array}$$
3.
$$\begin{array}{r} 6 \\ 4 \\ +\ 0 \\ \hline 10 \end{array}$$

4.
$$\begin{array}{r} 2 \\ 2 \\ +\ 3 \\ \hline 7 \end{array}$$

page 24
On Your Own: 34 laps

page 25
1. 22 yards
2. 32 cards
3. 27 holes
4. 92 runners

Unit 3

page 26
On Your Own: 1

page 27
1. 7
2. 2
3. 4
4. 3

page 28
On Your Own: 4
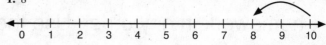

page 29
1. 8
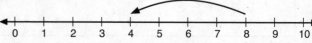

2. 4
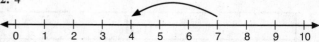

3. 5
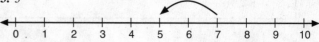

4. 7
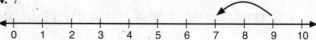

page 30
On Your Own: 2

page 31
1. 9
2. 3
3. 6
4. 16

page 32
On Your Own:
9, 1, 7, 8
8 − 1 = 7 should be circled.

page 33
1. 9, 8, 6, 2
   2 + 7 = 9 should be circled.
2. 8, 13, 3, 5
   8 + 5 = 13 should be circled.
3. 6, 4, 2, 4
   4 − 2 = 2 should be circled.
4. 13, 9, 5, 4
   9 + 4 = 13 should be circled.

page 34
On Your Own: 6

page 35
1. 3
2. 8
3. 5
4. 5

All-Star Math 1–2, SV 9781419099205

Unit 4

page 36

On Your Own:

Thousands	Hundreds	Tens	Ones
		2	0	9

page 37

1.

Thousands	Hundreds	Tens	Ones
3	2	0	4

2.

Thousands	Hundreds	Tens	Ones
1	8	2	6

3.

Thousands	Hundreds	Tens	Ones
	5	4	0

4.

Thousands	Hundreds	Tens	Ones
		6	8

page 38

On Your Own: 45 should be circled.

page 39

1. 10 should be circled.
2. 26 should be circled.
3. 11 should be circled.
4. 92 should be circled.

page 40

On Your Own: 24, 30; The rule is to count by 2s.

page 41

1. 69, 71; The rule is to count by 1s.
2. 20, 50; The rule is to count by 10s.
3. 21, 24; The rule is to count by 3s.

page 42

On Your Own: 4, 3; > should be circled.

page 43

1. 7, 8; < should be circled.
2. 10, 6; > should be circled.
3. 2, 5; < should be circled.
4. 8, 10; < should be circled.

Unit 5

page 44

On Your Own: The circle should be circled.

page 45

1. The cone should be circled.
2. The cube should be circled.
3. The cylinder should be circled.
4. The square should be circled.

page 46

On Your Own: The table-tennis paddles should be circled.

page 47

1. The ice skates should be circled.
2. The baseball caps should be circled.
3. The water skis should be circled.
4. The second and third ribbons should be circled.

page 48

On Your Own: The ice skate should be circled.

page 49

1. The baseball catcher's mitt should be circled.
2. The tennis shoe should be circled.
3. The bicycle should be circled.
4. The basketball should be circled.

page 50

On Your Own: 5 sides, 5 corners

page 51

1. 3 sides, 3 corners
2. 4 sides, 4 corners
3. 0 sides, 0 corners
4. 4 sides, 4 corners

page 52

On Your Own: Tennis shoe 1 should be circled.

page 53

1. The baseball player should be circled.
2. The sailboat should be circled.
3. The baseball bat should be circled.
4. The hockey player should be circled.

Unit 6

page 54

On Your Own: 120 yards should be circled.

page 55

1. 5 ounces should be circled.
2. 10 feet should be circled.
3. 31,000 gallons should be circled.
4. 1 inch should be circled.

page 56

On Your Own: 320 yards

page 57

1. 56 inches
2. 68 feet
3. 300 meters
4. 50 inches

page 58

On Your Own: Thermometer A

page 59

1. Thermometer A
2. Thermometer B
3. Thermometer B
4. Thermometer A

page 60

On Your Own: The shape showing 3 parts with 1 shaded part should be circled.

page 61

1. The shape showing 6 parts with 4 shaded should be circled.
2. The shape showing 4 parts with 3 shaded should be circled.
3. The shape showing 5 parts with 4 shaded should be circled.
4. The shape showing 3 parts with 2 shaded should be circled.

page 62

On Your Own: $\frac{1}{4}$ should be circled.

page 63

1. $\frac{1}{2}$ should be circled.
2. $\frac{2}{3}$ should be circled.
3. $\frac{3}{4}$ should be circled.
4. $\frac{3}{5}$ should be circled.

Unit 7

page 64

On Your Own: 4:15

page 65

1. 2:00
2. 5:00
3. 3:40
4. 11:45

page 66

On Your Own: June 7 and 8

page 67

1. June 30
2. June 5, 13, 19, and 25
3. June 8, 15, and 29
4. June 2

page 68

On Your Own: Answers may vary. 1 quarter, 3 dimes, 1 nickel, and 2 pennies could be colored.

page 69

1. 2 quarters, 2 dimes, and 2 nickels should be colored.
2. 1 dime, 1 nickel, and 4 pennies should be colored.
3. Answers may vary. 5 dimes, 2 nickels, and 7 pennies could be colored.
4. 2 quarters, 2 dimes, and 1 nickel should be colored.

page 70

On Your Own: Answers may vary. 3 nickels and 4 pennies, or 19 pennies are two possible answers.

page 71

1. 4 nickels and 3 pennies; or 23 pennies
2. 2 nickels and 2 pennies; or 12 pennies
3. 2 dimes, 1 nickel, and 1 penny; or 5 nickels and 1 penny; or 26 pennies
4. 8 pennies

page 72

On Your Own: 2¢

page 73

1. 33¢
2. 69¢
3. 55¢
4. 17¢

Unit 8

page 74
On Your Own: $3 + 3 + 3 + 3 = 12$; 4

page 75
1. $3 + 3 + 3 = 9$; 3
2. $2 + 2 = 4$; 2
3. $2 + 2 + 2 + 2 = 8$; 4
4. $6 + 6 + 6 = 18$; 3

page 76
On Your Own:
   a. $3 + 3 + 3 + 3 = 12$
   b. 4 groups of 3
   c. $4 \times 3 = 12$

page 77
1. a. $4 + 4 = 8$
   b. 2 groups of 4
   c. $2 \times 4 = 8$
2. a. $3 + 3 + 3 = 9$
   b. 3 groups of 3
   c. $3 \times 3 = 9$
3. a. $2 + 2 + 2 + 2 + 2 + 2 + 2 = 14$
   b. 7 groups of 2
   c. $7 \times 2 = 14$
4. a. $3 + 3 + 3 + 3 + 3 + 3 = 18$
   b. 6 groups of 3
   c. $6 \times 3 = 18$

page 78
On Your Own: 4

page 79
1. 4
2. 7
3. 8
4. 10

page 80
On Your Own: 3

page 81
1. 3
2. 7
3. 2

page 82
On Your Own: 2

page 83
1. 9
2. 4
3. 6
4. 10

Unit 9

page 84
On Your Own: 3

page 85
1. Stacy: 1 point
2. Kareem: 5 points
   Delia: 5 points
   Ling: 5 points
   Stacy: 5 points
3. 2 points
4. Kareem: 10 points

pages 86
On Your Own: 7 arrows

page 87
1. 1996
2. 1994: 25 cards
   1995: 45 cards
   1996: 50 cards
   1997: 45 cards
   1998: 5 cards
3. 5 cards
4. 20 cards

page 88
On Your Own: 5 home runs

page 89
1. Week 1: 400
   Week 2: 300
   Week 3: 300
   Week 4: 450
2. Week 4
3. Week 2 and Week 3
4. 1,450

page 91
1. The baseball should be circled.
2. The soccer ball should be circled.
3. The football should be circled.
4. The football should be circled.

page 92
On Your Own:

Win	Lose
Team 1	Team 2
Team 2	Team 1

page 93

1.

Morning	Afternoon
football	baseball
baseball	football

2.

First	Second
Dean	Sara
Sara	Dean

3.

First	Second
math	reading
reading	math

4.

First	Second	Third
Team 1	Team 2	Team 3
Team 1	Team 3	Team 2
Team 2	Team 1	Team 3
Team 2	Team 3	Team 1
Team 3	Team 1	Team 2
Team 3	Team 2	Team 1

All-Star Math 1–2, SV 9781419099205